FINDING LOVE AFTER INFIDELITY

Helpful tips on how to continue loving a partner after infidelity

Angela C. Bassett

TABLE OF CONTENT

CHAPTER 1

KNOWING WHAT TO DO

Don't blame yourself.

You could begin to feel inadequate, that you could have done more, loved more, or given more. In actuality, your efforts are sufficient. Maybe they discovered someone who has what they were seeking–something that you don't have or couldn't provide. Despite your best efforts, they determined they wanted something different. Nothing more you could have said or done would have caused him to change his mind. So, the fact that he cheated on you wasn't your fault.

Because infidelity isn't always clear, you might think that blaming yourself is the only reasonable course of action. Perhaps you believe that you have been aloof or haven't been very forthcoming in the bedroom. It's possible that you neglected the connection since job was taking up too much of your time. It's possible that these issues indicate that your relationship still needs work, but you should be aware that neither of these things will ever lead to your spouse's infidelity nor should you ever hold them responsible for their errors.

Certain issues in the relationship may be partially your responsibility, and it's crucial to accept that. However, you must never, ever believe that your own fault for your spouse's infidelity justifies it.
Your spouse will be released from responsibility if you place an excessive amount of emphasis on your faults. You should concentrate on your partner's actions as well.

Don't attempt to justify it

There's no point in attempting to make sense of absurdity, even if you might believe that if you can simply come up with a rational justification for why the cheating occurred, you'll be able to go on. Accept that you are upset and that you must find a method to get well, but don't imagine that blaming your partner will help you get past your problems.

It's possible that your spouse's reasoning for cheating was illogical. Don't spend too much time attempting to figure out the right explanation for what occurred; instead, focus on making progress.

Never reprimand your spouse.

Even while it may feel nice to treat your spouse badly, take away the things they enjoy, or even have an affair in retaliation, this type of conduct won't help you advance your relationship. You should avoid purposefully trying to make your spouse feel worse because doing so will only make you both feel worse. You can be hurt, cold, and keep your distance from your spouse for a while.

Punishing your partner will just increase your resentment and make your marriage feel even worse. It's acceptable to take some time away and act more distantly and icily than usual, but purposefully being harsh won't make anything better.

Avoid being fixated on the third party.

You may ask a gazillion questions about the other person, spend hours watching their Facebook page, or even try to get a sight of them in person if you want to drive yourself insane as rapidly as possible. Although you may believe that learning all there is to know about this person would help you understand what went wrong in your relationship, doing so will only make things worse for you.

Rarely does an affair involving a spouse involve a third party. Most of the time, unless that husband believes he has actually begun a genuine connection with a third person, it's really an expression of the cheater's dissatisfaction with himself or the marriage. If you focus too much on the other woman, then you won't be thinking about your spouse or the relationship.

Though knowing some things about the affair can bring you comfort, you may not want to know too much about what the other person looks like, what she does for a living, or any other details that are likely to distract you or to make you feel bad about yourself. It's just not worth it.

Don't obsess over what your friends and family will think.

You should keep what happened to yourself and not be concerned with what others who know about the affair may think. Although others close to you can offer you helpful advise, ultimately it comes down to what's best for you. If you decide to leave or stay in the relationship, you shouldn't worry about what other people will say. In the end, it doesn't matter what other people say, and you shouldn't allow their opinions to influence the choices you make.

Speaking with those who are close to you may undoubtedly provide you with strength and a fresh outlook on your circumstance. But in the end, remember that their views can never take the place of yours.

Don't tell the whole world

Your need to inform everyone in your family, your closest friends, or even to write about it on social media to truly get your thoughts out may come from a combination of extreme hurt and anger. For the rest of your life, you'll have to deal with people's perceptions of your spouse and your relationship if there's a chance that you want to make things work and reconcile. Tell just the individuals close to you who you believe can actually help you think things through, as opposed to telling everyone you know.

You could have some immediate comfort after telling everyone what occurred, but that relaxation might be followed by regret and anguish. It's possible that you were unprepared for everyone's opinions or criticism.

If you do decide to inform your close friends about your partner's infidelity, proceed with caution if you aren't sure what you want to do in response. If your friends believe you're about to break up with your boyfriend, they could list all the things they didn't like about him, which won't help you feel better and might make things unpleasant if you decide to stay.

Do not speak ill of your spouse

Never criticize your spouse in public. The two of you should continue to seem as one even while you are at odds. Speaking poorly of your spouse is the same as giving the opposition armor. It is also disrespectful to your spouse and your marriage.

This does not preclude you from venting to or confiding in your pals about your issues. Just be careful not to disparage your spouse or paint them as the villain.

CHAPTER 2

TAKING ACTION

Take time apart, if necessary.

It can be intense when you discover an affair. You may act out of anger or be in shock. Take some time away from your spouse to think about the affair and to process your emotions. Don't be afraid to give each other space if you think it will help you move past the infidelity.

Even if you really feel ready to forgive your spouse or for things to get back to normal, you should know that it can take a long time to regain that trust and loving feeling you once had for your spouse. Even if you're both determined to make it work, it can take a long time for things to feel, for lack of a better word, "normal" again, and for you to feel fondness toward the person you married. This is perfectly natural. If you try to rush things along you may run into trouble.

You won't be able to forgive your partner or to feel like things are back to normal overnight. It can take months, or even years, to rebuild that trust again.
You'll have to take it slow, too. It may take many days for you to feel comfortable sleeping in the same bed as your partner again, going out to dinner with him, or to enjoy doing the things you loved to do together. Be prepared for that

Reach out to family and friends

Look for objective, nonjudgmental support from friends, loved ones, or a spiritual leader. If you already have a therapist, you may want to reach out to them for professional guidance. Often it helps to have someone who will listen to you as you process your emotions and give you verbal or silent support as you deal with this intense event.

You can also lean on your family and friends as you continue to process and work through the infidelity. Once you decide to save your marriage and work through your issues with your spouse, it can be helpful to have a support network to turn to. It can be helpful to schedule time on the weekends to spend with family and friends as you work through the issues with your spouse

Embrace managing your own emotions even when they are overwhelming.

You may be shocked when your deep pain emerges. However, let your painful emotions matter to you — like feeling betrayed, rejected, worthless, unloved, disrespected, failed, etc. Attempt to make healthy choices around managing those emotions. You may experience disillusionment, rage, anger, grief, devastation, and depression. A professional counselor can help you manage this feeling.

Hate their actions, but not them

I realize this is difficult. But keep in mind that they used to be your entire existence. When no one else could, they stood by you. They too gave up a piece of themselves that they were unable to recover. Resentment won't serve you well if you harbor it toward them.

You won't feel any better as a result. People make errors, sometimes foolish and absurd ones. And the harsh reality is that, occasionally, just because someone makes a poor choice doesn't imply they are inherently evil.

Should You Give a Cheating Partner a Second Chance?

Giving a cheating spouse a second chance is one of the most difficult relationship decisions you hope to never have to make. This choice is particularly challenging if your partner lied to you, used deceit to their advantage, embarrassed you, or attempted to hide an affair.

But what if your mate is dependable and trustworthy most of the time? What if they decide they made a mistake and vow to remain faithful? What if you're certain that the two of you are in a romantic relationship? Everyone has their red line—the one thing that cannot be compromised. What that boundary is for you is something that only you know.

CHAPTER 3

CONDITIONS

Agreement

It may be advisable to stress that this is a one-time opportunity if you choose to offer your spouse another chance. They must comprehend that if they cheat once again, there would be no more opportunities.

Questions to Consider

Prior to giving your spouse another opportunity, it's crucial to consider all the steps that need to be taken to mend your relationship, including getting over the hurt, reestablishing trust, relearning how to be intimate, and enhancing communication. Here are some critical inquiries to make.

- Is this the first time your partner cheated on you?

- Does your partner recognize the harm they've done?
- Does your spouse acknowledge the issue with the cheating?
- Has your lover admitted to having been unfaithful?
- Will your partner acknowledge the need for behavioral adjustments, regardless of the circumstances surrounding the infidelity?
- Has your lover expressed regret?
- Do you think your lover regrets being unfaithful and is sincerely sorry?
- Will your partner go to individual and marital therapy?
- Have all connections to the involved party been severed?
- Have you spoken about how your partner can maintain the connection as a business-only one if the individual is someone your partner works with?
- Do you believe that your relationship with your spouse has the potential to be prosperous, happy, and lasting?

- Do you believe your lover will ever earn your trust again?
- Do you consider your marriage to be worth preserving?
- Do you believe that your partner's infidelity will always nag at your thoughts and emotions?
- Will you hold your partner's infidelity against them or are you able to forgive them?
- Are you thinking of getting back at them or gaining revenge?
- Are both of you ready to work on your relationship and figure out how to fix the underlying problems?

Answering these questions honestly can help you decide if you should give your partner a second chance. Look over your answers. Are they mostly positive? Or, are there areas that are cause for concern? You may want to discuss this list with a counselor or another neutral party who can help you evaluate your situation.

CHAPTER 4

REBUILDING YOUR RELATIONSHIP

Remember the good times

Spend some time reflecting about the good times you have had with your spouse. Think about how you fell in love, your dating experiences, your wedding, your honeymoon, the day you brought your first child home and all the other happy moments you have shared. Old photo albums, scrapbooks and journals can help to jog your memory.

Recalling good times helps to reignite the emotional connection you once shared with your spouse. It makes you want to create more happy memories with your spouse, which is the first step to falling in love again.

Express any hurt feelings honestly and openly

Expressing your emotions can help you gradually with the hurt and pain you are feeling. When you first discover the affair, it's important that you do not make any rash decisions. You will likely be very upset and hurt. Avoid letting your emotions dictate your reaction. Try to discuss the affair openly with your partner and focus on expressing how you are feeling, and try not yelling or screaming at each other. Let your spouse know what you're feeling. Tell him about the anger, the hurt, the betrayal, and the pain he has put you through. Don't keep your guard up and act like it wasn't that big of a deal; let him really see your pain and to hear how you're feeling. If you're not honest and open about what you're going through, then you won't ever be able to truly move forward together. Though you may feel shy or scared to reveal your true feelings, it's important that you do so.

If you're nervous about facing your spouse or not saying everything you wanted to say, you can write down all of the things you want to share. That way, you won't get lost in the moment and forget an important point you wanted to make.

If you feel too emotional to have a conversation about what happened, give it a few days or wait long enough to feel comfortable talking about it as candidly as possible. Of course, the conversation may never feel completely comfortable, but you can take some time to get your footing if you need to. That said, you may not want to delay this conversation for too long

Forgive your spouse

When someone cheats on you, you start to question your worth. Let me remind you that your worth is not determined by how others treat you, when you give someone all of that, you're giving a part of you that you cannot take back. Nobody deserves to be cheated on.

There is no way for your spouse to change the past or erase what happened. Therefore, if you want your marriage to work, you'll just have to find a way to forgive them. Holding on to anger, hurt or resentment will destroy any chance of a happy marriage.

Forgiveness is not fair, if you find yourself thinking that your spouse doesn't deserve forgiveness or hasn't done enough to make up for their mistake, remember that forgiveness frees you from the hurt and anger so that you can move on. Ask God to give you the grace to forgive your spouse.

Ask the questions that you want the answers to.

You may want some clarity when it comes to what your cheating spouse did. If you want to piece together how this has been going,then you can ask questions about how many times it happened, when it happened, how it started, or even about what your spouse feels about this other person. However, if you want there to be a chance that the relationship lasts, then you should think twice before asking about details that you may be better off not knowing.

Ask any questions that you think will help you get a better sense of where your relationship stands. However, try to avoid asking questions just to satisfy your curiosity; the answers may end up hurting too much.

Get medical testing.

As embarrassing as it may sound, as soon as you know that your spouse has cheated on you, you should both get tested immediately. You don't know what diseases the third party might have had, and you won't know whether or not this was passed on to you. Though your spouse may argue

that this isn't necessary, it's what you need to do to make sure you're both safe.
Going through this process will also help your spouse understand the gravity of his or her actions. Sleeping with someone else while also sleeping with you has put you at risk, and it's important to acknowledge that.

Listen to your spouse.

Though you will be feeling hurt, overwhelmed, betrayed, angry, and any number of other emotions that you want to let out, it's important to also sit and listen to your spouse. You may feel as if hearing him or her out is the last thing you want to do, but if you want to get some clarity and to move the relationship forward, then you have to hear his or her side of the story. You may learn about new feelings or frustrations that you didn't know your partner had.

It's not fair to think that he doesn't deserve to tell his side of the story or to have feelings in all this. Though you may not feel ready to confront your spouse's feelings, you have to let him express himself if you want to move forward

Improve your communication every day

Once you and your spouse have begun to talk about the cheating, you can work on improving your line of communication. Make sure to be open and honest, to talk regularly, and to avoid being passive aggressive as much as possible. Though this may seem impossible after what your spouse did, it's important to communicate as well as you can if you want things to get better.

Once you're up to it, make a point of meeting every day, pushing all distractions aside, and talking about how your relationship is going. If you feel like this is exhausting and only rehashing old feelings,

then you should work on talking more about the present and future than the past.
It's important that you and your spouse check in with each other to see how you're feeling. This is the time to be vigilant and to focus on your relationship. If you don't have strong communication, then it's hard to move forward.

Work on expressing your feelings with "I" statements, such as saying, "I feel sad when you don't greet me after you come home from work," instead of using "you" statements, such as, "You never give me any attention after you get home from work," which come off as more accusatory.

Spend time together, without bringing up the affair

If you want to start rebuilding your relationship, then you and your spouse should spend quality time together that has nothing to do with the fact that your spouse cheated. Work on doing the things you used to love together and avoiding the places that remind you of the cheating that took place. Make an effort to start from the bottom up, making sure your relationship has a solid foundation through daily activities before you move forward too fast.

You can even discover a new activity, such as hiking or cooking, to do together. This can help you see your relationship in a new light. Just make sure you don't feel like your partner is suffering through it or trying too hard.

Take care of yourself.

When you're dealing with a cheating spouse, you may feel like your last priority is to take care of yourself. You may be too busy feeling a whirlwind of complicated emotions to think about things like eating three meals a day, getting some sunshine, and making sure to get enough rest. However, if you want to stay strong during this difficult time and to have the energy to work on your relationship, then that is exactly what you have to do. Here are some things to keep in mind:

Try to get at least 7-8 hours of sleep per night. If you can't sleep because you're bothered by your spouse sleeping next to you, you should feel comfortable discussing alternative sleeping arrangements.
Work to eat three healthy meals a day. Though you may be prone to eating more

unhealthy foods, such as sugary snacks, because you're stressed, you should try to stay healthy to keep your spirits up. Fatty foods can make you feel sluggish.

Try to get at least 30 minutes of exercise a day. This time is good for your mind and body and can give you some time to be alone and not think about the affair.

Write in a journal. Try to write in it at least a few times a week to take some time to get in touch with your thoughts.

Don't isolate yourself. Spend more time with your friends and family to feel centered

Seek counseling

Relationships may survive infidelity, especially if your spouse is sincere in their regret. In fact, genuine regret is a strong sign that the relationship still has a chance, especially if you've been together for a while and have kids together.

But you both need to understand that things will never be the same in your relationship. If you want things to change, you can't just act like nothing ever occurred. To make the relationship work, you both need to put in a lot of effort.

Counseling isn't for everyone, but if you're trying to save your marriage, you and your spouse should give it a go. The best way to establish a safe environment for you and your partner so that you can truly feel comfortable sharing your feelings is by doing this. You may feel like it will be too embarrassing or too much for you, but it may actually be the best way. Find a therapist you can depend on, and give your sessions your best.

Make it plain to your partner that you will not back out if this is essential to you. Your spouse should be able to take care of things for you because they betrayed your trust.

www.ingramcontent.com/pod-product-compliance
Lightning Source LLC
LaVergne TN
LVHW020538160826
845677LV00015B/4130
9798847839990